RECORDER FUN!™

T0070496

Disney
CINDERELLA
MUSIC FROM THE MOTION PICTURE SOUNDTRACK

CONTENTS

2 **GETTING STARTED**

4 **READING MUSIC**

8 **FINGERING CHART**

SONGS

10 **BIBBIDI-BOBBIDI-BOO (THE MAGIC SONG)**

12 **A DREAM IS A WISH YOUR HEART MAKES**

15 **THE FIRST BRANCH**

17 **A GOLDEN CHILDHOOD**

19 **SEARCHING THE KINGDOM**

21 **THE SLIPPER**

22 **STRONG**

24 **VALSE ROYALE**

ISBN 978-1-4950-2618-8

Walt Disney Music Company

DISTRIBUTED BY

HAL•LEONARD®
CORPORATION

7777 W. BLUEMOUND RD. P.O. BOX 13819 MILWAUKEE, WI 53213

In Australia Contact:
Hal Leonard Australia Pty. Ltd.
4 Lentara Court
Cheltenham, Victoria, 3192 Australia
Email: ausadmin@halleonard.com.au

Visit Hal Leonard Online at
www.halleonard.com

GETTING STARTED

HOLDING THE RECORDER

Here is how to hold the recorder. The mouthpiece rests on your lower lip, just like a drinking straw, with only a little of it actually going inside your mouth. Be sure that all of the finger holes line up on the front of the recorder as shown in the picture.

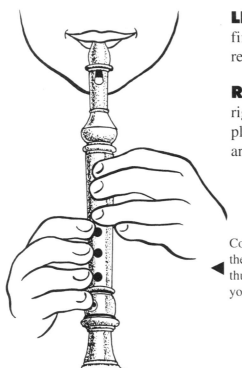

LEFT HAND — The first three fingers of your left hand (the little finger is not used) play the *top* three holes on the front of the recorder. The thumb of your left hand plays the hole on the back.

RIGHT HAND — The *bottom* four holes are played by your right-hand fingers. There is no hole for your right-hand thumb to play so it can help hold the recorder steady while the other fingers are busy playing.

◀ Cover the top three holes with your left-hand fingers and the bottom four holes with your right-hand fingers. The thumb of your left hand covers the hole in the back of your recorder.

MAKING A SOUND

To make a sound on the recorder blow gently into the small opening at the top of the mouthpiece. You can change this sound by covering different holes with your thumb and fingers. For example, when you cover all of the thumb and finger holes you will get a low, quiet sound. When only one or two holes are covered the sound will be higher and much louder.

Here are some tips for getting the best possible sound out of your recorder:

Always blow gently into the mouthpiece — Breathe in and then gently blow into the mouthpiece as if you were sighing or using a straw to blow out a candle. Remember, always blow gently.

Leaks cause squeaks — Play the holes using the pads of your fingers and thumb (not the tips). Press against each hole firmly so that it is completely covered and no air can sneak out. Even a tiny leak of air will change a beautiful tone into a sudden squeak!

Use your tongue to start each tone — Place your tongue against the roof of your mouth just behind your front teeth and start each tone that you play by tonguing the syllable "du" or "too" as you blow gently into the recorder.

PLAYING A TONE

Musical sounds are called *tones*. Every tone has a letter name. *Finger charts* are used to show you exactly which holes should be covered in order to play a particular tone. Each circle on these charts represents one of the holes on your recorder. The thumb hole is represented by the circle to the left of the recorder in the chart.

●   means that you should cover that hole.

○   means that that hole should not be covered but left open.

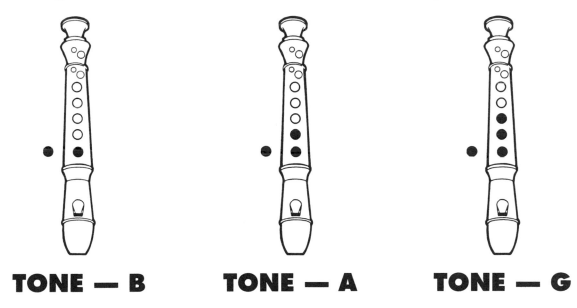

TONE — B   **TONE — A**   **TONE — G**

Use these three tones to play "Mary Had A Little Lamb:"

MARY HAD A LITTLE LAMB

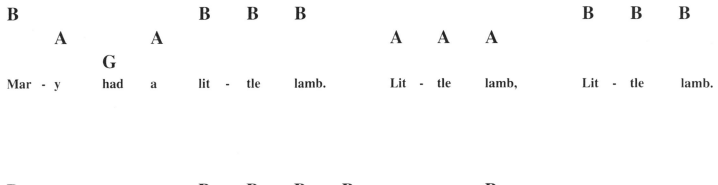

B				B	B	B						B	B	B
	A		A					A	A	A				
		G												
Mar - y		had	a	lit -	tle	lamb.		Lit -	tle	lamb,		Lit -	tle	lamb.

B				B	B	B	B				B	
	A		A					A	A		A	
		G										G
Mar - y		had	a	lit -	tle	lamb	whose	fleece	was	white	as	snow.

READING MUSIC

Musical notes are an easy way to see everything that you need to know in order to play a song on your recorder:

How high or low — Notes are written on five lines that are called a *staff*. The higher a note is written on the staff the higher it will sound.

How long or short — The color of a note (black or white) tells you if it should be played short or long. The black notes in "Mary Had A Little Lamb" are all one beat long (*quarter notes*). The first three white notes in this song are two beats long (*half notes)* and the last note is four beats long (*whole note*).

How the beats are grouped — The two numbers at the beginning of the song (4/4) are called a *time signature*. This time signature tells you that the *beats* in this song are grouped in fours: **1** 2 3 4 **1** 2 3 4 etc. To help you see this grouping, *bar lines* are drawn across the staff to mark each *measure* of four beats. A *double bar* is used to mark the end of the song.

Now here is how "Mary Had A Little Lamb" looks when it is written in musical notes:

MARY HAD A LITTLE LAMB

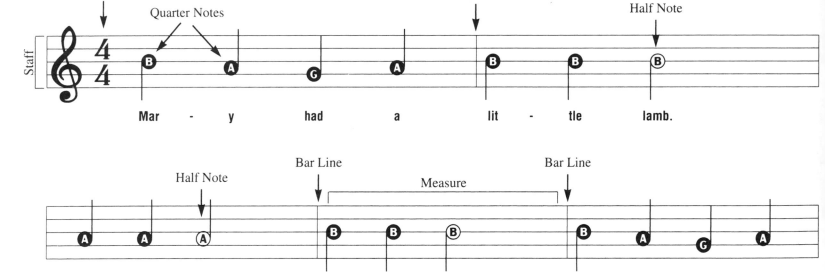

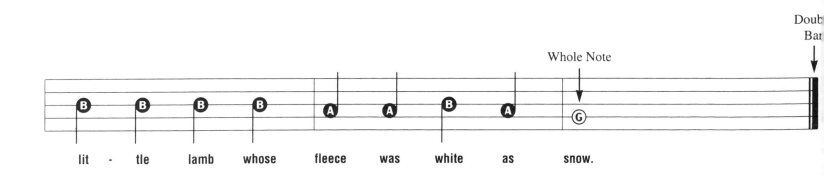

TWO NEW TONES

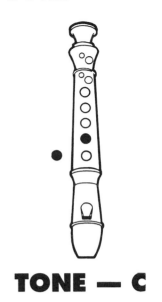 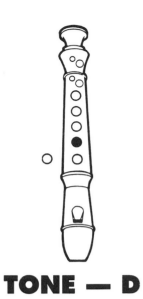

TONE — C **TONE — D**

AURA LEE

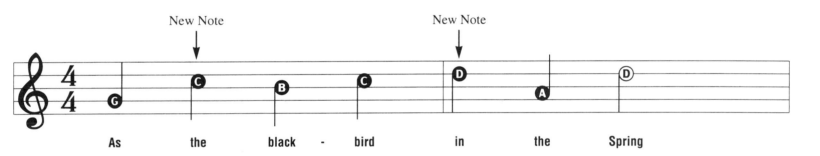

New Note   New Note

As   the   black - bird   in   the   Spring

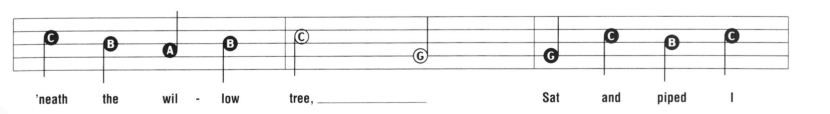

'neath   the   wil - low   tree, _____   Sat   and   piped   I

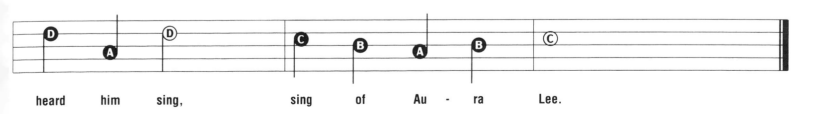

heard   him   sing,   sing   of   Au - ra   Lee.

USING YOUR RIGHT HAND

"Twinkle, Twinkle Little Star" uses the tone E. As you can see from the fingering chart, you will use three fingers of your left hand and two fingers of your right to play this tone. The thumb hole is only half filled in (◖). This means that you should "pinch" the hole with your thumb so that only a small part of the hole is left open. Pinching is done by bending your thumb so that the thumbnail points directly into the recorder leaving the top of the thumb hole open.

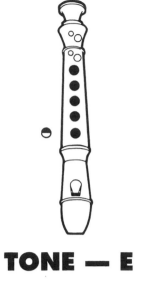

TONE — E

TWINKLE, TWINKLE LITTLE STAR

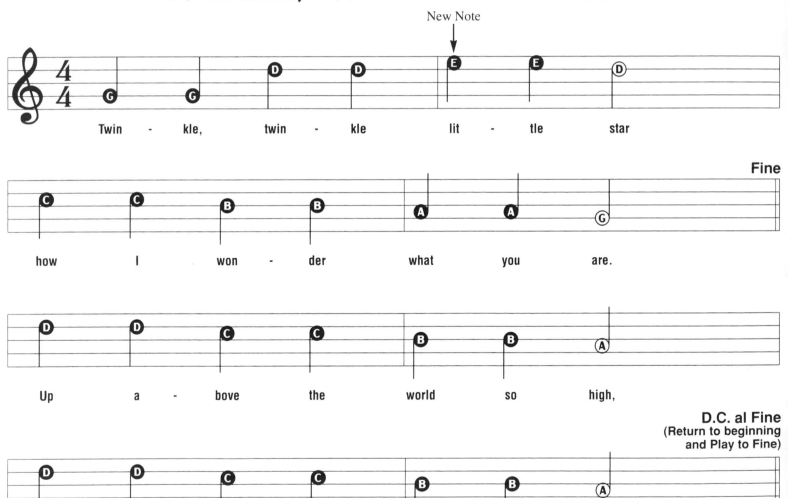

Copyright © 1992 by HAL LEONARD PUBLISHING CORPORATION
International Copyright Secured   All Rights Reserved

NOTES AND RESTS

In addition to notes that are one, two or four beats long, other values are possible. Also, *rests* are used to indicate when you should *not* play a tone but be silent. The chart on page 7 will help you identify the different notes and rests that are used in this book.

COUNT:

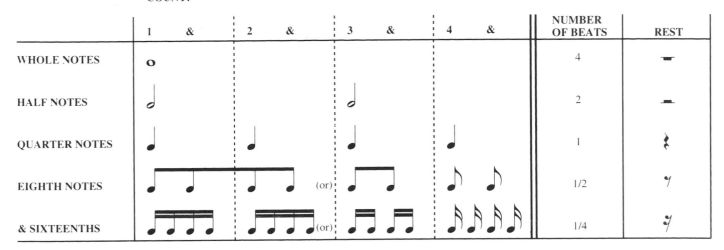

DOTTED NOTES ARE 1 1/2 TIMES THE NORMAL LENGTH:

TRIPLETS ARE SPREAD EVENLY ACROSS THE BEATS:

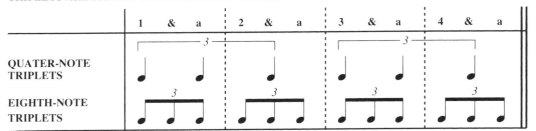

THIS OLD MAN

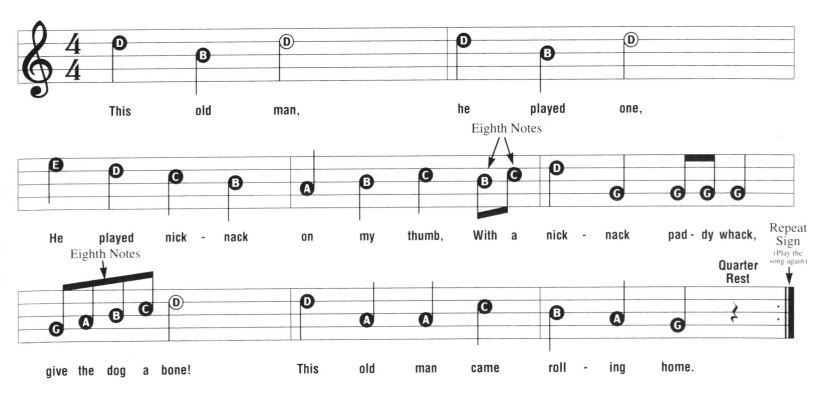

FINGERING CHART

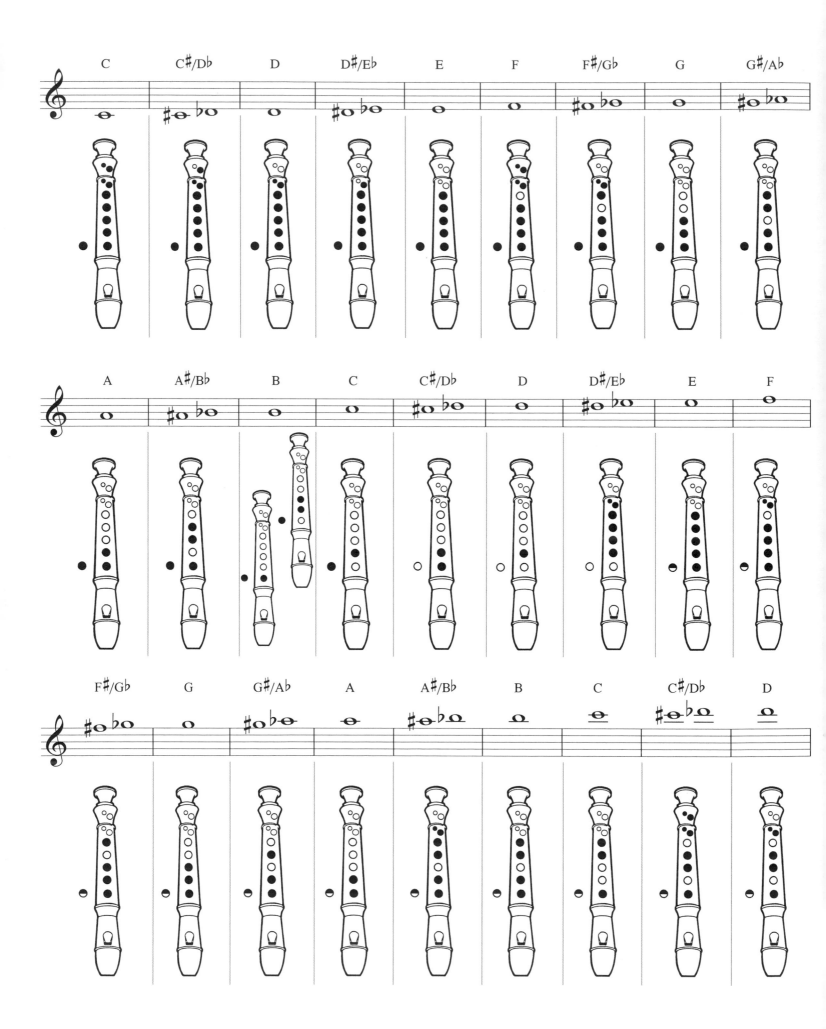

BIBBIDI-BOBBIDI-BOO
(THE MAGIC SONG)

Words by Jerry Livingston
Music by Mack David and Al Hoffman

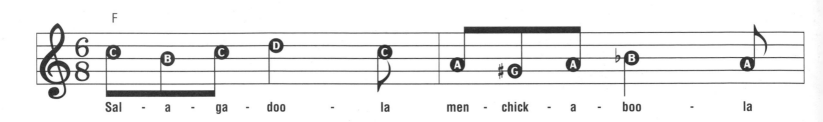

Sal - a - ga - doo - la men - chick - a - boo - la

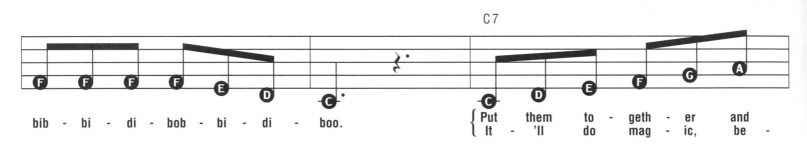

bib - bi - di - bob - bi - di - boo. Put them to - geth - er and
It - 'll do mag - ic, be -

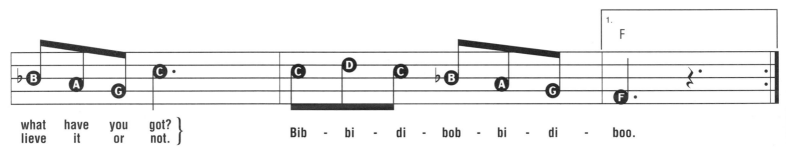

what have you got?
lieve it or not. Bib - bi - di - bob - bi - di - boo.

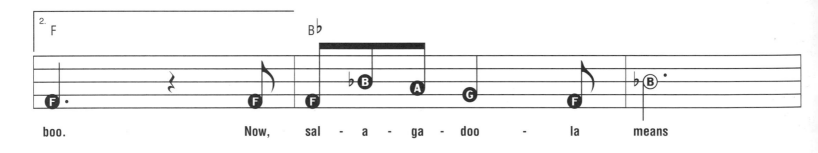

boo. Now, sal - a - ga - doo - la means

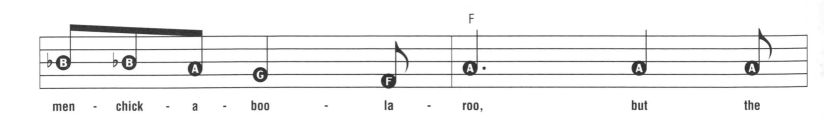

men - chick - a - boo - la - roo, but the

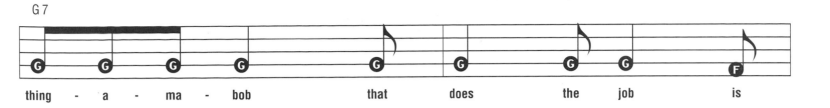

G 7

thing - a - ma - bob   that   does   the   job   is

C 7   F

bib - bi - di - bob - bi - di - boo.   Sal - a - ga - doo - la

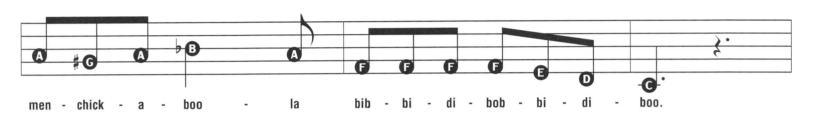

men - chick - a - boo - la   bib - bi - di - bob - bi - di - boo.

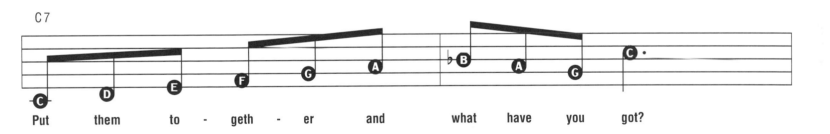

C 7

Put   them   to - geth - er   and   what   have   you   got?

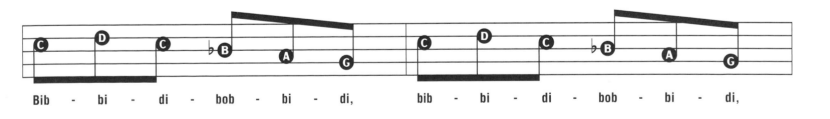

Bib - bi - di - bob - bi - di,   bib - bi - di - bob - bi - di,

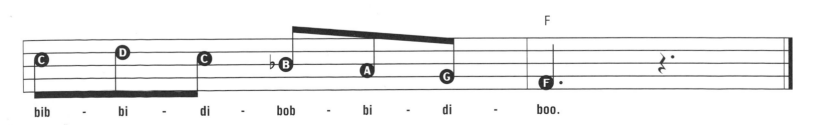

F

bib - bi - di - bob - bi - di - boo.

A DREAM IS A WISH YOUR HEART MAKES

Words and Music by Mack David,
Al Hoffman and Jerry Livingston

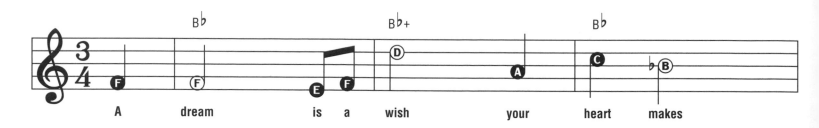

A dream is a wish your heart makes

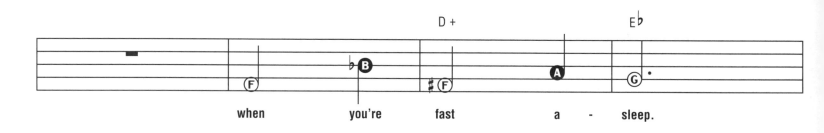

when you're fast a - sleep.

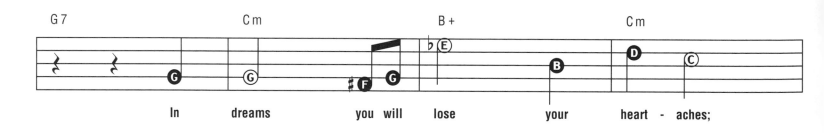

In dreams you will lose your heart - aches;

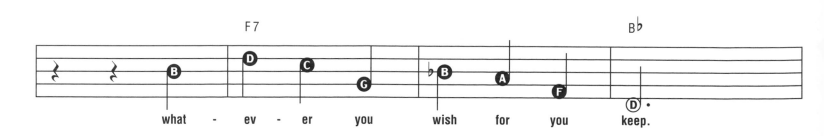

what - ev - er you wish for you keep.

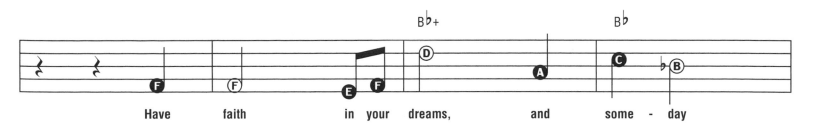

Have faith in your dreams, and some - day

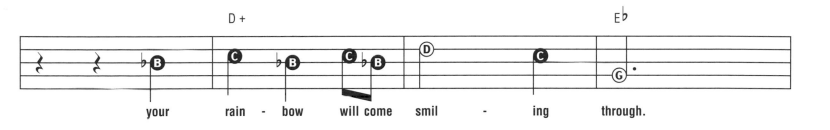

your rain - bow will come smil - ing through.

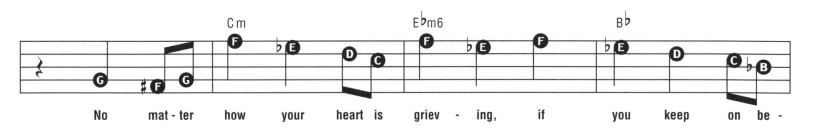

No mat - ter how your heart is griev - ing, if you keep on be -

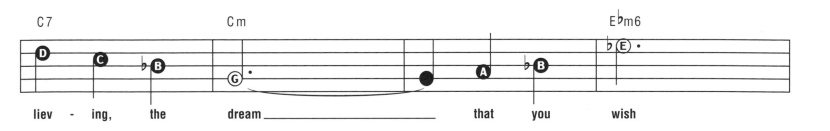

liev - ing, the dream _____ that you wish

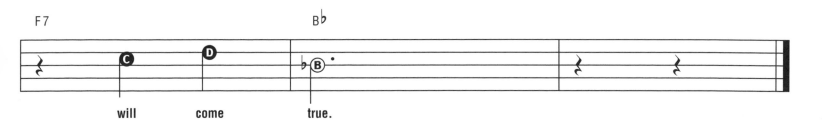

will come true.

THE FIRST BRANCH

Music by Patrick Doyle

A GOLDEN CHILDHOOD

Music by Patrick Doyle

SEARCHING THE KINGDOM

Music by Patrick Doyle

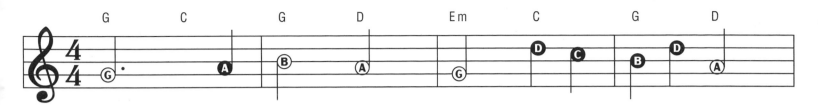

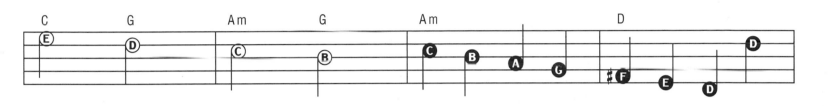

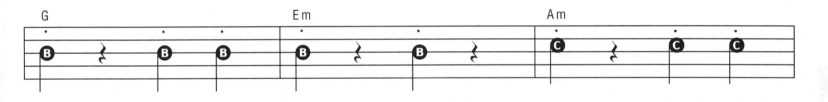

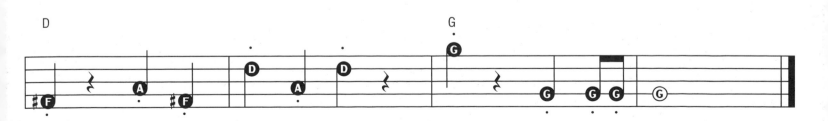

THE SLIPPER

Music by Patrick Doyle

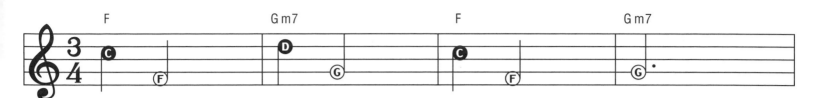

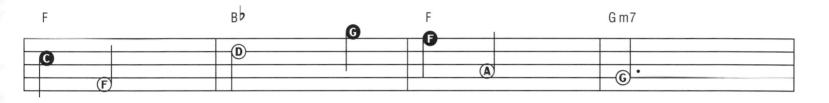

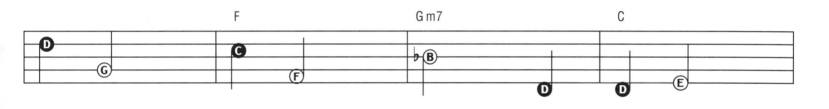

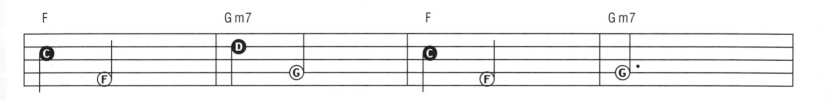

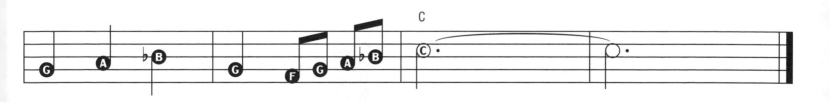

STRONG

Words and Music by Patrick Doyle,
Kenneth Branagh and Tommy Danvers

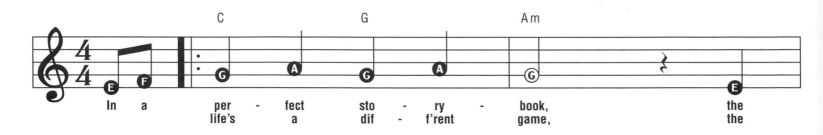

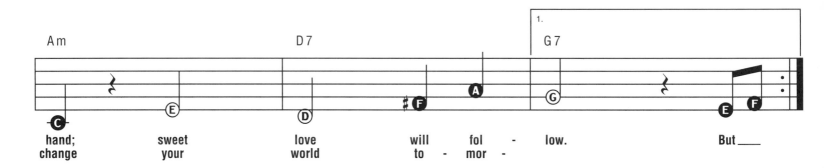

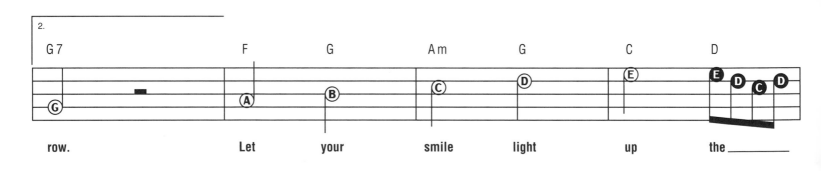

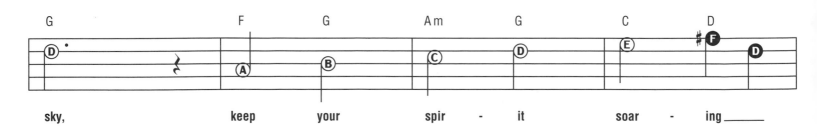

23

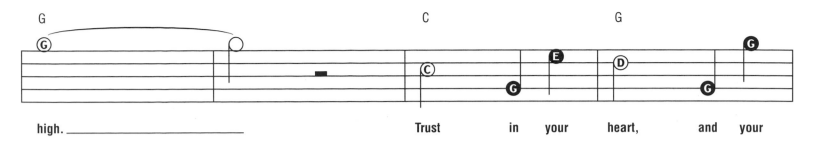

high. _____ Trust in your heart, and your

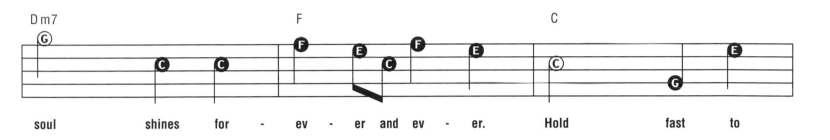

soul shines for - ev - er and ev - er. Hold fast to

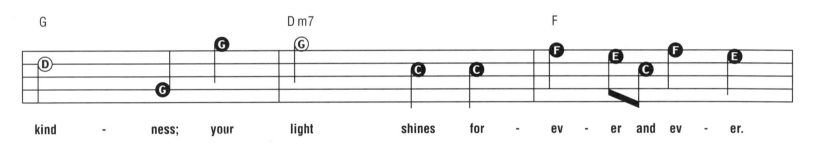

kind - ness; your light shines for - ev - er and ev - er.

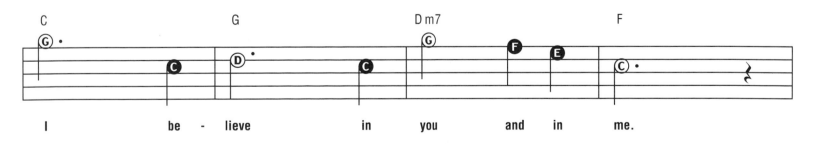

I be - lieve in you and in me.

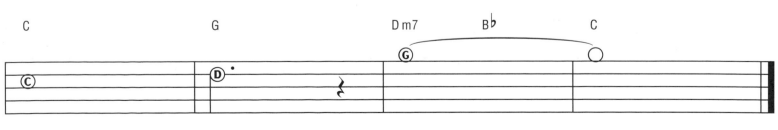

We are strong. _____

VALSE ROYALE

Music by Patrick Doyle

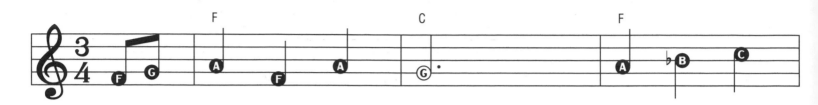

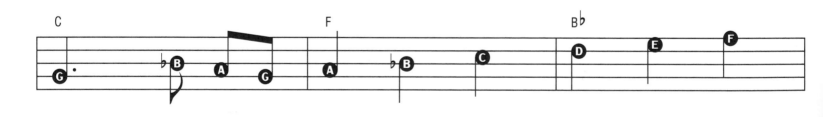

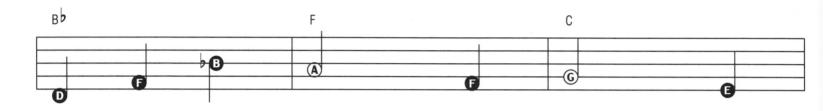

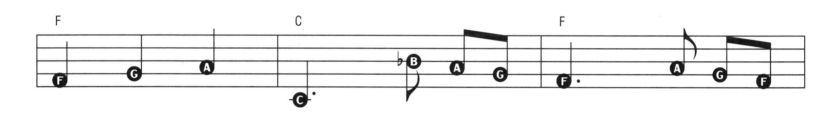